TO

Ate Cindy

FROM

I Love you ate.
Ranson Liam

DATE

Oct. 16, 2010

bigidea.com

VeggieTales®

30 VERY VEGGIE DEVOS ABOUT HONESTY

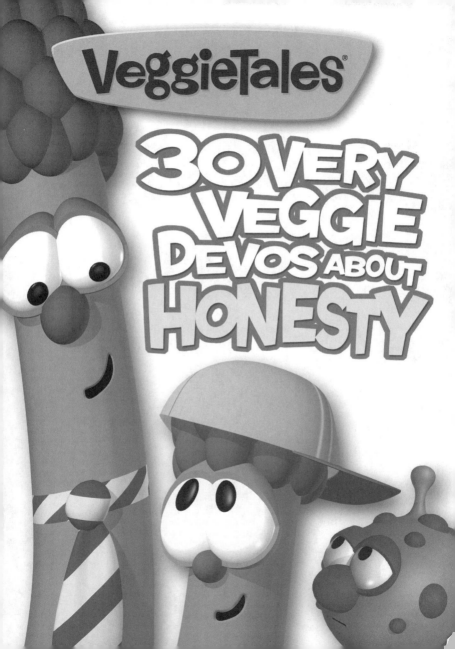

VeggieTales®

30 VERY VEGGIE DEVOS ABOUT HONESTY

TABLE OF CONTENTS

A MESSAGE FOR PARENTS

If you're already familiar with VeggieTales®, you know the importance of providing your youngster with a steady stream of big ideas from God's Word. And this VeggieTales® devotional book can help you do just that.

This little text contains 30 brief chapters, one for each day of the month. Each chapter consists of a Bible verse, a brief story or lesson, kid-friendly quotations from notable Christian thinkers, a timely tip, and a prayer. Every chapter examines a different aspect of an important Biblical theme: honesty.

So please try this experiment: For the next 30 days, take the time to read one chapter each night to your child, and then spend a few moments talking about the chapter's meaning. By the end of the month, you will have had 30 different opportunities to share God's wisdom with your son or daughter, and that's good . . . very good.

If you have been touched by God's love and His grace, then you know the joy that He has brought into your own life. Now it's your turn to share His message with the boy or girl whom He has entrusted to your care. Happy reading! And may God richly bless you and your family now and forever.

A MESSAGE FOR KIDS

Have you seen the VeggieTales® episode called *LarryBoy and the Fib from Outer Space?* If so, you probably remember how a very little fib turned into a very big problem for Junior Asparagus. How big was that problem? Well, what started out as a tiny little lie quickly turned in to a 30-foot tall monster! And the same thing that happened to Junior can happen to you. If you tell a fib, it's likely to grow, and fast. That's why the big ideas in this book—ideas about what it means to tell the truth—are really important.

So for the next month, ask your mom or dad to help you read a chapter a day. When you do, you'll soon figure out that honesty is always the best policy . . . and that's the truth!

Good people
will be guided by honesty.

Proverbs 11:3 ICB

DAY 1

IT'S IMPORTANT TO BE HONEST

Good people will be guided by honesty.

Proverbs 11:3 ICB

It's important to be honest. When you tell the truth, you'll feel better about yourself, and other people will feel better about you, too. But that's not all. When you tell the truth, God knows—and He will reward you for your honesty.

Telling the truth is hard sometimes. But it's better to be honest, even when it's hard. So remember this: telling the truth is always the right thing to do . . . always.

We must constantly strive to keep
our integrity intact. When wealth is lost,
nothing is lost; when health is lost,
something is lost;
when character is lost, all is lost.

Billy Graham

God doesn't expect you to be perfect,
but he does insist on complete honesty.

Rick Warren

TODAY'S BRIGHT IDEA

If you know what's right and do what's right,
you'll be a happier person. Honest and good
behavior make you happier—and bad behavior
doesn't. Behave accordingly.

PRAYER OF THE DAY

Dear Lord, help me be a person whose
words are true and whose heart is
pure. In everything that I do,
let me use Jesus as my model
and my guide, today and always.
Amen

DAY 2

THE BEST POLICY

In every way be an example
of doing good deeds.

Titus 2:7 NCV

Maybe you've heard this phrase: "Honesty is the best policy." And, of course, it is the best policy, but more importantly, it is also God's policy.

If we want to please God, we must honor Him by obeying His commandments. He has commanded us to be honest with everybody. Truth is God's way, and it must be our way, too.

A lie is like a snowball:
the further you roll it,
the bigger it becomes.

Martin Luther

Honesty has a beautiful and refreshing
simplicity about it. No ulterior motives.
No hidden meanings. As honesty and integrity
characterize our lives, there will be
no need to manipulate others.

Charles Swindoll

TODAY'S BRIGHT IDEA

Honesty is the best policy. Make sure that it's
your policy, even when telling the truth makes
you feel a little uncomfortable.

PRAYER OF THE DAY

Dear Lord, the Bible teaches me
that honesty is the best policy.
Help me remember that lesson
today and every day of my life.
Amen

DAY 3

CRYING "WOLF!"

Innocent people will be kept safe.
but those who are dishonest
will suddenly be ruined.
Proverbs 28:18 ICB

Perhaps you've heard the story of the boy who cried "wolf!" In that story, the boy exaggerated his problems and eventually got himself into BIG trouble!

When we pretend that our troubles are worse than they really are, we may earn a little sympathy now, but we'll invite lots of trouble later.

If you're ever tempted to cry "wolf!," don't. Exaggeration wasn't good for the boy who cried "wolf!," and it's not good for you.

Truth is always exciting.
Speak it, then. Life is dull without it.

Pearl Buck

Truth is the only safe ground to stand upon.

Elizabeth Cady Stanton

TODAY'S BRIGHT IDEA

Don't Exaggerate! All of us have enough troubles without pretending that we have more.

PRAYER OF THE DAY

Dear Lord, let me always remember that none of my problems are ever too big for You!
Amen

WHEN MISTAKES HAPPEN

But if we confess our sins, he will forgive our sins. We can trust God. He does what is right. He will make us clean from all the wrongs that we have done.

1 John 1:9 ICB

Do you make mistakes? We all do. Nobody is perfect, and you should not expect to be perfect, either. When you make a mistake, the best thing to do is to admit it, to correct it, and to try very hard not to make it again. Then, your mistakes can become opportunities to learn.

Sometimes, mistakes can be the very best way to learn, so learn from them. But don't keep making the same mistake over and over again. That's not learning; that's silly!

Father, take our mistakes
and turn them into opportunities.
Max Lucado

God is able to take mistakes, when they
are committed to Him, and make of them
something for our good and for His glory.
Ruth Bell Graham

TODAY'S BRIGHT IDEA

Fix it sooner rather than later: If you make
a mistake or say something that isn't true,
the time to make things better is now, not
later! The sooner you admit your mistake, the
better.

PRAYER OF THE DAY

Dear Lord, when I make mistakes,
let me admit them and correct them.
When I am wrong, let me be quick to
change and quick to ask forgiveness
from others and from You.
Amen

DAY 5

HONESTY
IS A HABIT!

We must not become tired of doing good.
Galatians 6:2 ICB

Our lives are made up of lots and lots of habits. And the habits we choose help determine the kind of people we become. If we choose habits that are good, we are happier and healthier. If we choose habits that are bad, then it's too bad for us!

Honesty, like so many other things, is a habit. And it's a habit that is right for you.

Do you want to grow up to become the kind of person that God intends for you to be? Then get into the habit of being honest with everybody. You'll be glad you did . . . and so will God!

The simple fact is that if we sow
a lifestyle that is in direct disobedience
to God's revealed Word,
we ultimately reap disaster.

Charles Swindoll

You can build up a set of good habits
so that you habitually take the Christian way
without thought.

E. Stanley Jones

TODAY'S BRIGHT IDEA

Choose all your habits carefully: habits are
easier to make than they are to break, so be
careful!

PRAYER OF THE DAY

Dear Lord, help me to be an honest
person all the time, not just some of
the time. And let the things that
I say and do be pleasing to You
this day and every day.
Amen

DAY 6

GROWING UP
WITH GOD

He will teach us of his ways,
and we will walk in his paths.

Isaiah 2:3 KJV

When will you stop growing up? Hopefully never! If you keep studying God's Word and obeying His commandments, you will never be a "fully grown" Christian. You will always be a "growing" Christian.

An important part of growing up is learning that honesty is better than dishonesty and that true words are better than lies. You have already learned that lesson; now, it's time to put your knowledge to good use by doing the things that you know are right.

God knows you can't be perfect, but He doesn't want you to keep doing bad things, either! Instead, God wants you to keep growing in the love and knowledge of His Son. When you do, you'll keep on growing, and that's exactly the kind of Christian that God wants you to become.

God loves us the way we are,
but He loves us too much to
leave us that way.

Leighton Ford

With God, it isn't who you were
that matters; it's who you are becoming.

Liz Curtis Higgs

TODAY'S BRIGHT IDEA

Daily Devotionals? Yes! Try your best to read
the Bible with your parents every day. If they
forget, remind them!

PRAYER OF THE DAY

Dear Lord, let me always keep
learning about Your love and about
Your Son, Jesus. Make me a better
person today than I was yesterday,
and let me continue to grow as
a Christian every day that I live.
Amen

SOMETIMES IT'S HARD

I asked the Lord for help,
and he answered me.
He saved me from all that I feared.

Psalm 34:4 ICB

Telling the truth can be hard sometimes. But even when telling the truth is very hard, that's exactly what you should do. If you're afraid to tell the truth, pray to God for the courage to do the right thing, and then do it!

If you've ever told a big lie, and then had to live with the big consequences of that lie, you know that it's far more trouble to tell a lie than it is to tell the truth. But lies aren't just troubling to us; they're also troubling to God! So tell the truth, even when it's hard to do; you'll be glad you did . . . and so will He!

Help yourself and God will help you.
St. Joan of Arc

Pray as if it's all up to God,
work as if it's all up to you.
Anonymous

TODAY'S BRIGHT IDEA

When it's hard to tell the truth: When telling
the truth is hard, that probably means that
you're afraid of what others might think—or
what they might do—when you're truthful.
Remember that it is usually better to face
those kinds of problems now rather than later!

PRAYER OF THE DAY

Dear Lord, let me tell the truth,
even when telling the truth is hard.
Give me the courage and the wisdom
to be honest with my family and with
my friends, today and every day.

Amen

WHAT THE BIBLE SAYS

Your word is like a lamp for my feet
and a light for my way.

Psalm 119:105 ICB

What book contains everything that God has to say about honesty? The Bible, of course. If you read the Bible every day, you'll soon be convinced that honesty is very important to God. And, since honesty is important to God, it should be important to you, too.

The Bible is the most important book you'll ever own. It's God's Holy Word. Read it every day, and follow its instructions. If you do, you'll be safe now and forever.

Jesus loves me! This I know,
for the Bible tells me so.
Little ones to him belong; they are weak,
but he is strong. Yes, Jesus loves me!
The Bible tells me so.

Anna B. Warner and Susan Warner

If you'll flip from cover to cover,
you'll notice that it's overwhelmingly
a book of stories—tales of men and women
who walked with God.

John Eldredge

TODAY'S BRIGHT IDEA

Who's in charge of your Bible? If you're the
person who's supposed to be taking care
of your Bible, then take the responsibility
seriously. Your Bible is by far the most
important book you own!

PRAYER OF THE DAY

Dear Lord, You have given me
a wonderful gift: the Holy Bible.
Let me read it and understand it
and follow the commandments
that I find there.
Amen

DAY 9

DOING WHAT'S RIGHT

Doing what is right brings freedom
to honest people.

Proverbs 11:6 ICB

Doing the right thing isn't always easy, especially when we're tired or frustrated. But, doing the wrong thing almost always leads to trouble. And sometimes, it leads to BIG trouble.

When you do the right thing, you don't have to worry about what you did or what you said. But, if you are dishonest—or if you do something that you know is wrong—you'll be worried that someone will find out. So do the right thing; it may be harder in the beginning, but it's easier in the end.

There may be no trumpet sound or loud applause when we make a right decision, just a calm sense of resolution and peace.

Gloria Gaither

Preach the gospel at all times and, if necessary, use words.

St. Francis of Assisi

TODAY'S BRIGHT IDEA

If you're not sure what to do . . . ask yourself this question: "Would I be embarrassed if somebody found out?" If the answer is "Yes," don't do it!

PRAYER OF THE DAY

Dear Lord, teach me to be a truthful,
kind, generous person every day that
I live. Let me live by Your rules,
and let me accept the love of
Your Son, now and forever.
Amen

LISTENING TO YOUR CONSCIENCE

Believe me, I do my level best to keep
a clear conscience before God
and my neighbors in everything I do.

Acts 24:16 MSG

Sometimes, you know that something isn't the right thing to do, but you do it anyway. Even if no one else knows, you know . . . and so does God! You can keep secrets from other people, but you can't keep secrets from Him. God knows what you think and what you do.

If your heart tells you not to do something, don't do it! If your conscience tells you that something is wrong, stop! If you're tempted to say something that isn't true, don't! You can keep secrets from other people some of the time, but God is watching all of the time, and He sees everything, including your heart.

God desires that we become spiritually
healthy enough through faith to have
a conscience that rightly interprets
the work of the Holy Spirit.

Beth Moore

A quiet conscience sleeps in thunder.

Thomas Fuller

TODAY'S BRIGHT IDEA

That little voice inside your head . . . is called
your conscience. Listen to it; it's usually right!

PRAYER OF THE DAY

Dear Lord, other people see me
only from the outside, but You know
my heart. Let my heart be pure,
and let me listen to the voice that
You have placed there,
today and every day that I live.
Amen

WHEN WE'RE NOT HONEST

Dishonesty will destroy those
who are not trustworthy.

Proverbs 11:3 ICB

Have you ever said something that wasn't true? When you did, were you sorry for what you had said? Most likely so.

When we're dishonest, we make ourselves unhappy in surprising ways. Here are just a few troubles that result from dishonesty: we feel guilty and we are usually found out and we disappoint others and we disappoint God. It's easy to see that lies always cause more problems than they solve.

Happiness and honesty always go hand in hand. But it's up to you to make sure that you go hand in hand with them!

Those who walk in truth walk in liberty.
Beth Moore

Truth will triumph.
The Father of truth will win,
and the followers of truth will be saved.
Max Lucado

TODAY'S BRIGHT IDEA

Did you tell a lie? Apologize and make it right!
Did you say something that was untrue? Then
it's time to make things right by telling the
truth. It's never too late to tell the truth, but
it's never too early, either!

PRAYER OF THE DAY

Dear Lord, when I make mistakes,
help me to correct them.
And then, Lord, help me to not make
those same mistakes again.
Let me become wiser each day
so that I can become the kind of
Christian that You want me to be.
Amen

THE TROUBLE WITH GOSSIP

A person who gossips ruins friendships.

Proverbs 16:28 ICB

Do you know what gossip is? It's when we say bad things about people who are not around to hear us. When we say bad things about other people, we hurt them and we hurt ourselves. That's why the Bible tells us that gossip is wrong.

When we say things that we don't want other people to know we said, we're being somewhat dishonest, but if the things we say aren't true, we're being very dishonest. Either way, we have done something that we will regret later, especially if the other person finds out.

So do yourself a big favor: don't gossip. It's a waste of words, and it's the wrong thing to do. You'll feel better about yourself if you don't gossip about other people. So don't do it!

We should have great peace if we did not
busy ourselves with what others say and do.
Thomas à Kempis

To belittle is to be little.
Anonymous

TODAY'S BRIGHT IDEA

Don't say something behind someone's back
that you wouldn't say to that person's face.

PRAYER OF THE DAY

Dear Lord, make me a person who
says the same things to other people
that I say about them. Make my words
helpful, encouraging, and true.
And let the light of Christ shine in me
and through me, today and forever.
Amen

BEING HONEST AND WORRYING LESS

It is better to be poor and honest
than to be foolish and tell lies.

Proverbs 19:1 ICB

When we tell a lie, the trouble starts. Lots of trouble. But when we tell the truth—and nothing but the truth—we stop Old Man Trouble in his tracks.

When we always tell the truth, we make our worries smaller, not bigger. And that's precisely what God wants us to do.

So, if you would like to have fewer worries and more happiness, abide by this simple rule: tell the truth, the whole truth, and nothing but the truth. When you do, you'll make many of your worries disappear altogether. And that's the truth!

Worry is the senseless process of
cluttering up tomorrow's opportunities
with leftover problems from today.
Barbara Johnson

Worry is a complete waste of energy.
It solves nothing. And it won't solve
that anxiety on your mind either.
Charles Swindoll

TODAY'S BRIGHT IDEA

Worried about something you said or did? If
you made a mistake yesterday, the day to fix it
is today. Then, you won't have to worry about
it tomorrow.

PRAYER OF THE DAY

Dear Lord, if I make a mistake,
let me correct it. If I say something
that is untrue, let me apologize.
If I behave badly, let me correct
my bad behavior. Let me do the best
I can, Lord, and then let me leave
the worrying up to You.
Amen

WHEN FRIENDS MISBEHAVE

Hate what is evil.
Hold on to what is good.

Romans 12:9 ICB

When your friends misbehave or say things that aren't true, do you tell them to stop, or do you go along with the crowd? Usually, it's much easier to go along with the crowd—or to say nothing at all—but that's the wrong thing to do. It's better to stand up for what you know is right.

Sometimes, grownups must stand up for the things they believe in. When they do, it can be hard for them, too. But the Bible tells us over and over again that we should do the right thing, not the easy thing.

God's world is a wonderful place, but people who misbehave can spoil things in a hurry. So if your friends behave poorly, don't copy them! Instead, do the right thing. You'll be glad you did . . . and so will God!

Those who follow the crowd usually
get lost in it.

Rick Warren

True friends will always lift you higher
and challenge you to walk in
a manner pleasing to our Lord.

Lisa Bevere

TODAY'S BRIGHT IDEA

If you're not sure that it's the right thing to
do, don't do it! And if you're not sure that it's
the truth, don't tell it.

PRAYER OF THE DAY

Dear Lord, today I will worry less
about pleasing other people
and more about pleasing You.
Amen

GOD KNOWS

I am the Lord, and I can look
into a person's heart.

Jeremiah 17:10 ICB

Even when you think nobody is watching, God is. Nothing that we say or do escapes the watchful eye of our Lord. God understands that we are not perfect, but He also wants us to live according to His rules, not our own.

The next time that you're tempted to say something that you shouldn't say or to do something that you shouldn't do, remember that you can't keep secrets from God. So don't even try!

Bible history is filled with people who began the race with great success but failed at the end because they disregarded God's rules.

Warren Wiersbe

Don't worry about what you do not understand. Worry about what you do understand in the Bible but do not live by.

Corrie ten Boom

TODAY'S BRIGHT IDEA

Made a mistake? Ask for forgiveness? If you've broken one of God's rules, you can always ask Him for His forgiveness. And He will always give it!

PRAYER OF THE DAY

Dear Lord, thank You for watching over me. Let the things that I say and do be pleasing to You. And Lord, thank You for Your love; let me share it with others today and every day.

Amen

SOONER OR LATER, THE TRUTH COMES OUT!

Everything that is hidden will be shown.
Everything that is secret will be made known.

Luke 12:2 ICB

How often do lies stay hidden? Not very often. Usually, the truth has a way of coming out, and usually it comes out sooner rather than later. That's one of the reasons that it's so silly to tell lies: lying simply doesn't work!

Truth, on the other hand, works extremely well. When you tell the truth, you don't have to remember what you said, and there's nothing bad for other people to find out. So do yourself a favor and get into the habit of telling the truth about everything. Otherwise, you'll be letting yourself in for a whole lot of trouble, and you'll be letting yourself in for it soon!

Every decision God makes is a good and
right decision, so we can be certain
that every decision God makes regarding us
will be a right one.

Bill Hybels

God is in control of history; it's His story.
Doesn't that give you a great peace—
especially when world events seem
so tumultuous and insane?

Kay Arthur

TODAY'S BRIGHT IDEA

You've got a secret? Probably not! Keeping
lies hidden is usually impossible, so why even
try?

PRAYER OF THE DAY

Dear Lord, sooner or later,
the truth has a way of coming out.
So give me the wisdom and the
courage to tell the truth in the very
beginning. The truth is Your way,
Lord; let be it my way, too.
Amen

THE RULE THAT'S GOLDEN

Do for other people the same things
you want them to do for you.

Matthew 7:12 ICB

Do you want other people to be honest with you? Of course you do. And that's why you should be honest with them. The words of Matthew 7:12 remind us that, as believers in Christ, we should treat others as we wish to be treated. And that means telling them the truth!

The Golden Rule is your tool for deciding how you will treat other people. When you use the Golden Rule as your guide for living, your words and your actions will be pleasing to other people and to God.

The Golden Rule starts at home,
but it should never stop there.

Marie T. Freeman

Anything done for another is
done for oneself.

Pope John Paul II

TODAY'S BRIGHT IDEA

Use the Golden Rule to help you decide what
to say: If you wouldn't like something said
about you, then you probably shouldn't say it
about somebody else!

PRAYER OF THE DAY

Dear Lord, help me remember to
treat other people in the same way
that I would want to be treated
if I were in their shoes.
The Golden Rule is Your rule,
Father; I'll make it my rule, too.
Amen

WHAT WOULD JESUS SAY?

So Jesus said to the Jews who believed
in him, "If you continue to obey
my teaching, you are truly my followers."

John 8:31 ICB

I f you are tempted to say something that isn't true, stop and ask yourself a simple question: "What would Jesus say if He were here?" The answer to that question will tell you what to say.

Jesus told His followers that the truth would make them free. As believers, we must do our best to know the truth and to tell it. When we do, we behave as our Savior behaved, and that's exactly how God wants us to behave.

A disciple is a follower of Christ.
That means you take on His priorities as
your own. His agenda becomes your agenda.
His mission becomes your mission.

Charles Stanley

We have in Jesus Christ a perfect example
of how to put God's truth into practice.

Bill Bright

TODAY'S BRIGHT IDEA

Learn from your Bible: Start learning about
Jesus, and keep learning about Him as long
as you live. His story never grows old, and His
teachings never fail.

PRAYER OF THE DAY

Dear Lord, the Bible is Your gift to me.
Let me use it, let me trust it,
and let me obey it, today
and every day that I live.
Amen

DAY 19

THAT BELONGS TO SOMEONE ELSE!

You must not steal.

Exodus 20:15 ICB

Have you ever been tempted to take something that didn't belong to you? If you did steal, you probably felt bad about doing so, and with good reason. We all know that it's wrong to take things that don't belong to us, but sometimes we do it anyway. Why? Because we aren't strong enough or smart enough not to.

God's plan for your life does not include stealing, so don't do it. Ever.

If it belongs to somebody else, don't take it. Don't even think about taking it! Don't even think about thinking about taking it. Don't even think about thinking about thinking about . . . oh well, you get the point!

Discontent dries up the soul.

Elisabeth Elliot

As a moth gnaws a garment,
so does envy consume a man.

St. John Chrysostom

TODAY'S BRIGHT IDEA

Want something? Ask, don't take! It's okay to ask. It's not okay to take!

PRAYER OF THE DAY

Dear Lord, help me to turn away
from dishonesty so that I can live in
the comfort of Your truth,
now and forever.
Amen

THE BLAME GAME

Lead a quiet and peaceable life
in all godliness and honesty.

1 Timothy 2:2 KJV

When something goes wrong, do you look for somebody to blame? And do you try to blame other people even if you're the one who made the mistake? Hopefully not!

It's silly to try to blame other people for your own mistakes, so don't do it.

If you've done something you're ashamed of, don't look for somebody to blame; look for a way to say, "I'm sorry, and I won't make that same mistake again."

When a man points a finger at someone else,
he should remember that four of his fingers
are pointing at himself.

Louis Nizer

When you blame others,
you give up your power to change.

Anonymous

TODAY'S BRIGHT IDEA

Don't play the blame game: it's very tempting
to blame others when you make mistakes or
say something that isn't true. But it's more
honest to look in the mirror first.

PRAYER OF THE DAY

Dear Lord, when I make a mistake,
I want to admit it. Help me not blame
others for the mistakes that I make.
And when I make a mistake,
help me to learn from it.
Amen

SOLOMON SAYS

Keep your eyes focused on what is right.
Keep looking straight ahead to what is good.

Proverbs 4:25 ICB

I n the Book of Proverbs, King Solomon gave us wonderful advice for living wisely. Solomon said that we should keep our eyes "focused on what is right." In other words, we should do our best to say and do the things that we know are pleasing to God.

The next time you're tempted to say an unkind word or to say something that isn't true, remember the advice of King Solomon. Solomon said that it's always better to do the right thing, even when it's tempting to do otherwise.

So if you know something is wrong, don't do it; instead, do what you know to be right. When you do, you'll be saving yourself a lot of trouble and you'll be obeying the Word of God.

When we do what is right, we have
contentment, peace, and happiness.
Beverly LaHaye

Learning God's truth and getting it into
our heads is one thing, but living God's truth
and getting it into our characters is
quite something else.
Warren Wiersbe

TODAY'S BRIGHT IDEA

Simon says? Solomon says! Have you ever
played the game Simon Says? When you play it,
you're not supposed to move until the leader
calls out, "Simon Says!" Wise King Solomon
had many rules for living. You should get to
know those rules—especially the ones found
in the Book of Proverbs. Then, you can be
guided by the things that Solomon says!

PRAYER OF THE DAY

Dear Lord, let me grow up to become
wise. Let me study Your Word
and learn Your ways so that I can
become the kind of Christian
that You want me to be.
Amen

DAY 22

LITTLE LIES
GROW UP!

The honest person will live in safety,
but the dishonest will be caught.

Proverbs 10:9 NCV

Sometimes, people can convince themselves that it's okay to tell "little white lies." And, sometimes people convince themselves that itsy bitsy lies aren't harmful. But there's a problem: little lies have a way of growing into big ones, and once they grow up, they cause lots of problems.

Remember that lies, no matter what size, are not part of God's plan for our lives, so tell the truth about everything. It's the right thing to do, and besides: when you always tell the truth, you don't have to try to remember what you said!

It is twice as hard to crush a half-truth
as a whole lie.

Austin O'Malley

Those who are given to white lies
soon become color blind.

Author unknown

TODAY'S BRIGHT IDEA

Think first! Think before you say things . . .
Slow down long enough to think about the
things you're about to do or say. That way,
you'll make better choices.

PRAYER OF THE DAY

Dear Lord, help me to turn away from
dishonesty so that I can live in
the comfort of Your truth,
now and forever.
Amen

DAY 23

IT'S YOUR DECISION

Lord, teach me what you want me to do.
And I will live by your truth.

Psalm 86:11 ICB

Nobody can tell the truth for you. You're the one who decides what you are going to say. You're the one who decides whether your words will be truthful . . . or not.

The word "integrity" means doing the right and honest thing. If you're going to be a person of integrity, it's up to you. If you want to live a life that is pleasing to God and to others, make integrity a habit. When you do, everybody wins, especially you!

Don't worry about what you do not understand. Worry about what you do understand in the Bible but do not live by.

Corrie ten Boom

Make all your decisions in the light of Jesus Christ.

Oswald Chambers

TODAY'S BRIGHT IDEA

It's a choice: Being an honest person is a choice. And if you're smart, you'll make it your choice.

PRAYER OF THE DAY

Dear Lord, help me to make decisions
that are pleasing to You. Help me be
honest, patient, and kind. And help me
to follow the teachings of Jesus,
not just today, but every day.
Amen

DAY 24

IT'S EASIER TO TELL THE TRUTH

The goodness of an innocent person
makes his life easier.

Proverbs 11:5 ICB

Sometimes, telling the truth is hard to do, but even then, it's easier to tell the truth than it is to live with the consequences of telling a lie. You see, telling a lie can be easier in the beginning, but it's always harder in the end! In the end, when people find out that you've been untruthful, they may feel hurt and you will feel embarrassed.

So make this promise to yourself, and keep it: don't let lies rob you of your happiness. Instead, tell the truth from the start. You'll be doing yourself a big favor, and you'll be obeying the Word of God.

Fill the heart with the love of Christ
so that only truth and purity can
come out of the mouth.

Warren Wiersbe

In all your deeds and words,
you should look on Jesus as your model,
whether you are keeping silence or speaking,
whether you are alone or with others.

St. Bonaventure

TODAY'S BRIGHT IDEA

If a little lie gets started, nip it in the bud: it's
always easier to stop a tiny lie before it has
had a chance to grow up into a very big lie!
Telling the truth stops the lie from growing.

PRAYER OF THE DAY

Dear Lord, let me be honest about
big things and about little things.
When I tell the truth, my life is better
and my conscience is clear,
so let me tell the truth and live it,
today and every day.
Amen

DAY 25

BEING A TRUSTWORTHY FRIEND

Tell each other the truth because
we all belong to each other . . . .

Ephesians 4:25 ICB

All genuine friendships are built upon both honesty and trust. Without trust, friends soon drift apart. But with trust, friends can stay friends for a lifetime.

As Christians, we should always try to be trustworthy, encouraging, loyal friends. And, we should be thankful for the people who are loyal friends to us. When we treat other people with honesty and respect, we not only make more friends, but we also keep the friendships we've already made.

Do you want friends you can trust? Then start by being a friend they can trust. That's the way to make your friendships strong, stronger, and strongest!

The best times in life are made
a thousand times better
when shared with a dear friend.

Luci Swindoll

You can make more friends in two months
by becoming more interested in other people
than you can in two years by trying to
get other people interested in you.

Dale Carnegie

TODAY'S BRIGHT IDEA

Lies tear down trust: one of the best ways
to destroy even a friendship is to lie to your
friend . . . so don't do it!

PRAYER OF THE DAY

Dear Lord, help me to be
an honest friend. Since I want other
people to be truthful with me,
let me be truthful with them,
today and every day.
Amen

HONESTY AT HOME

You must choose for yourselves today whom
you will serve . . . as for me and my family,
we will serve the Lord.

Joshua 24:15 NCV

Should you be honest with your parents? Certainly. With your brothers and sisters? Of course. With cousins, grandparents, aunts, and uncles? Yes! In fact, you should be honest with everybody in your family because honesty starts at home.

If you can't be honest in your own house, how can you expect to be honest in other places, like at church or at school? So make sure that you're completely honest with your family. If you are, then you're much more likely to be honest with everybody else.

If you tell the truth, you don't have to
remember anything.

Mark Twain

Having truth decay? Brush up on your Bible!

Anonymous

TODAY'S BRIGHT IDEA

Talk about your feelings: If something is
bothering you, tell your parents. Don't be
afraid to talk about your feelings. Your mom
and dad love you, and they can help you. So
whatever "it" is, talk about it . . . with your
parents!

PRAYER OF THE DAY

Dear Lord, help me be honest
with everybody, especially my family
members. Make my words true
and helpful, now and always.
Amen

HONESTY AT SCHOOL

Being respected is more important
than having great riches.

Proverbs 22:1 ICB

If you are going to school, you already know that it's important to tell the truth when you are in the classroom. And, you know that it's not right to take things that are not yours.

Of course, some children will behave dishonestly, and soon everyone will know what they have done. Other children will behave honestly, and soon everyone will know that the honest kids can be trusted.

What kind of student do you want to be? Do you want to be a person who is respected, or not? Do you want to be a person who is trusted, or not? The choice is yours, and the choice should be obvious.

To stand in an uncaring world and say,
"See, here is the Christ"
is a daring act of courage.

Calvin Miller

We need to talk to God about people,
then talk to people about God.

Dieter Zander

TODAY'S BRIGHT IDEA

Put it back! If, in a moment of weakness, you
take something that isn't yours, put it back
. . . now!

PRAYER OF THE DAY

Dear Lord, I know that it's important
to be an honest person. Since I want
other people to be truthful with me,
let me be truthful with them,
today and every day.
Amen

BEING HONEST AND KIND

Don't ever stop being kind and truthful.
Let kindness and truth show in all you do.

Proverbs 3:3 ICB

Honesty and kindness should go hand in hand. In other words, we shouldn't use honesty as an excuse to hurt other people's feelings.

It's easy to find faults in other people, and easy to tease other people about their shortcomings. But it's wrong. When we needlessly hurt other people's feelings, we are disobeying God.

The Bible tells us that we should never stop being kind and truthful. And, that's very good advice for caring, thoughtful Christians . . . like you!

Do all the good you can. By all the means you can. In all the ways you can. In all the places you can. At all the times you can. To all the people you can. As long as ever you can.

John Wesley

Showing kindness to others is one of the nicest things we can do for ourselves.

Janette Oke

TODAY'S BRIGHT IDEA

Don't be cruel: Sometimes, you can be too honest, especially if you say unkind things that are intended to hurt other people's feelings. When you're deciding what to say, you should mix honesty and courtesy. When you do, you'll say the right thing.

PRAYER OF THE DAY

Dear Lord, help me to be a person
who is both honest and kind.
Let my words be truthful
and encouraging. Let me always
remember the Golden Rule,
and let me speak accordingly.
Amen

THE TRUTH ACCORDING TO JESUS

So Jesus said to the Jews who believed
in him, "If you continue to obey my
teaching, you are truly my followers.
Then you will know the truth.
And the truth will make you free."

John 8:31-32 ICB

Jesus had a message for all of His followers. He said, "The truth will set you free." When we do the right thing and tell the truth, we don't need to worry about our lies catching up with us. When we behave honestly, we don't have to worry about feeling guilty or ashamed. But, if we fail to do what we know is right, bad things start to happen, and we feel guilty.

Jesus understood that the truth is a very good thing indeed. We should understand it, too. And, we should keep telling it as long as we live.

Freedom is not the right to do what we want
but the power to do what we ought.

Corrie ten Boom

Real freedom means to welcome
the responsibility it brings, to welcome
the God-control it requires, to welcome
the discipline that results, to welcome
the maturity it creates.

Eugenia Price

TODAY'S BRIGHT IDEA

The Truth with a capital "T": Jesus is the
Truth with a capital "T" . . . and that's the
truth!

PRAYER OF THE DAY

Dear Lord, thank You for
Your Son Jesus. Let Him be the light
of my life, the Savior of my soul,
and the model for my behavior.
Amen

DAY 30

HONESTY STARTS WITH YOU!

These are the things you must do:
Speak truth to one another; render honest
and peaceful judgments in your gates.

Zechariah 8:16 HCSB

Where does honesty begin? In your own heart and your own head. If you sincerely want to be an honest person, then you must ask God to help you find the courage and the determination to be honest all of the time.

Honesty is not a "sometimes" thing. If you intend to be a truthful person, you must make truthfulness a habit that becomes so much a part of you that you don't have to decide whether or not you're going to tell the truth. Instead, you will simply tell the truth because it's the kind of person you are.

Lying is an easy habit to fall into, and a terrible one. So make up your mind that you're going to be an honest person, and then stick to your decision. That's what your parents want you to do, and that's what God wants, too. And since they love you more than you know, trust them. And always tell the truth.

The health of anything—whether
a garden plant or a heart devoted to God—
reflects what is going on
(or not going on!) underground.

Elizabeth George

The more wisdom enters our hearts,
the more we will be able to trust
our hearts in difficult situations.

John Eldredge

TODAY'S BRIGHT IDEA

How can you please your Heavenly Father? By
telling the truth, by obeying your parents, and
by obeying God.

PRAYER OF THE DAY

Dear Lord, I know that it's important
to be an honest person.
Since I want other people to be
truthful with me, let me be
truthful with them,
today and every day.
Amen

BIBLE VERSES
TO MEMORIZE

For God so loved the world,
that He gave His only begotten Son,
that whoever believes in Him
shall not perish,
but have eternal life.

John 3:16 NASB

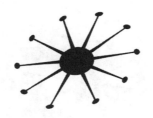

We must not become tired of doing good.

Galatians 6:2 ICB

The thing you should want most is
God's kingdom and doing what
God wants. Then all these other things
you need will be given to you.

Matthew 6:33 ICB

Lord, teach me what you
want me to do.
And I will live by your truth.

Psalm 86:11 ICB

I am not alone, because the Father is with Me.

John 16:32 HCSB

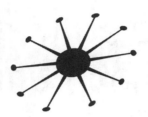

You must choose for yourselves
today whom you will serve . . .
as for me and my family,
we will serve the Lord.

Joshua 24:15 NCV

Be still, and know that I am God....

Psalm 46:10 KJV

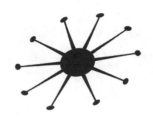

A person who gossips ruins friendships.

Proverbs 16:28 ICB

I can do all things through Christ which strengtheneth me.

Philippians 4:13 KJV

Tell each other the truth because we all belong to each other . . . .

Ephesians 4:25 ICB

The Lord is the strength of my life.

Psalm 27:1 KJV

I am the Lord, and I can look into a person's heart.

Jeremiah 17:10 ICB

The Lord is my shepherd,
I shall not want.
He makes me lie down
in green pastures;
He leads me beside quiet waters.
He restores my soul.

Psalm 23:1-3 NASB

Good people will be guided by honesty.

Proverbs 11:3 ICB

Fear not,
for I am with you.

Isaiah 41:10 NKJV

Blessed is he that trusts in the Lord.

Proverbs 16:20 NIV

Don't ever stop being kind
and truthful.
Let kindness and truth
show in all you do.

Proverbs 3:3 ICB

Lead a quiet and peaceable life in all godliness and honesty.

1 Timothy 2:2 KJV

You shall not steal, nor deal falsely, nor lie to one another.

Leviticus 19:11 NASB

I have given you
an example to follow.
Do as I have done to you.

John 13:15 NLT

We love Him because He first loved us.

1 John 4:19 NKJV